Children Support Plans and its Link to Quality of Care

Child and Adolescent Studies

Alero George-Taylor

authorHOUSE®

AuthorHouse™ UK
1663 Liberty Drive
Bloomington, IN 47403 USA
www.authorhouse.co.uk
Phone: 0800.197.4150

Published by AuthorHouse 04/30/2019

ISBN: 978-1-7283-8747-5 (sc)
ISBN: 978-1-7283-8746-8 (e)

Print information available on the last page.

Any people depicted in stock imagery provided by Getty Images are models, and such images are being used for illustrative purposes only. Certain stock imagery © Getty Images.

This book is printed on acid-free paper.

Because of the dynamic nature of the Internet, any web addresses or links contained in this book may have changed since publication and may no longer be valid. The views expressed in this work are solely those of the author and do not necessarily reflect the views of the publisher, and the publisher hereby disclaims any responsibility for them.

*Dedication to my wonderful parents for
being my biggest role models and showing
me that believing in myself is the first secret
to success and ultimate happiness.*

*Secondly to my amazing Husband for not only
loving me unconditionally, but always being
my motivator and true best friend.
Love you dearly.*

*My last dedication would be to children and
young people in care all around the world for
their strengths and abilities to conquer and
positivity in their transition from childhood into
adulthood and ultimately making a difference
as extra ordinary individuals in the society.*

CONTENTS

PREFACE

This book analyses the complex relationship between the support plans in place for children looked after (CLA) and their quality of care. In the provision of care and support for all children, there are national (UK) and international (United Nations) guidelines laid down, not only in achieving the five outcomes outlined in the document "Every Child Matters" but also in achieving equality and human rights for every child, as enshrined in the United Convention for the Rights of the Child. This research will explore the extent to which these guidelines have ensured the quality of care provided to CLA aligned with the provisions in these guidelines. The book critically analyses the quality of care provided to CLA, employing the "four Ps" as tools of analysis (participation, protection, prevention, and provision) as outlined in the Child Rights Convention (CRC). By using this framework, the book shows the importance of the four Ps in providing a high quality of care and support to CLA.

ACKNOWLEDGEMENTS

Foremost, I acknowledge the grace of God for making it possible to complete this research despite several challenges during the whole process. Secondly, I thank my family for their genuine love and support, without which the project would not have been possible.

And the final acknowledgment is to all my readers for taking time to read my book.

CHAPTER 1

INTRODUCTION

"Within the Convention on the Rights of the Child (UNCRC) the United Nations has given the global community an international instrument of high quality protecting the dignity, equality and basic human rights of the world's children" (UNICEF, 2014).

This convention's definition of "child" or "young person" covers the period starting at conception. It includes anyone in need of special safeguarding and care because of his physical and mental immaturity, thereby including appropriate legal protection before and after birth. On the other hand, Article 41 does not interfere with any legislation or law concerning the rights of a child if the national law provides better protection for the child's rights. Furthermore, the definition of a child in Article 1 states that a child is a person below the age of 18 unless the laws of a particular country set a younger legal age for adulthood (UNICEF, 2014).

Article 2 of the UNCRC (non-discrimination) states that regardless of race, age, religion, abilities, disabilities, native language, domicile, income, and so on, no child or young person should be treated unfairly at any point in time (Newell, 1991). Also, the core rights and freedoms of children and young people are set out in the European Convention on Human Rights (ECHR). It details children's right to privacy; as well as freedom of expression of thought, conscience, and religion, which were incorporated in domestic law through the Human Rights Act of 1998 (HRA, 1998). The Children Act 1989 aimed to ensure that the welfare of the child is paramount, working in partnership with parents to protect the child from harm. The act is intended to strengthen a child's legal position to give him or her equal rights, ensure that their feelings and wishes are considered, and ensure the child is consulted and kept informed about their rights. The Children Act 2004 aims to further improve children's lives and gives the legal underpinning to Every Child Matters, which strives for change concerning children (2004).

There have been a few structural changes in response to the Children Act 2004, which have been brought together under a director of children's services in each local authority (The New Working Together to Safeguard Children 2013). This "New Working Together" streamlines previous guidance to clarify the responsibilities of professionals towards safeguarding children and redirecting the focus from processes and onto the needs of the child. It is paramount that all children have a right to participate in the decision-making process in all aspects of their lives; for example, where they want to live and, in some cases, where they want to go to school or college. Article 12 of the UNCRC states that it fully grants a child rights who is capable of forming a view and expressing that view freely in all matters affecting him or her, and these views should be given due consideration in accordance with the age and maturity of the child (Bell, 2012).

What is the definition of "children looked after (CLA)"? According to the National Society for the Prevention for the Cruelty to Children (NSPCC, 2014), the terms "children looked after" and "young people" are generally used to mean those looked after by the state, according to relevant national legislation, which differs among England, Northern Ireland, Scotland, and Wales. The term "CLA" can also be described as accommodated children and young people who are looked after voluntarily at the request of, or by agreement with, their parents. These children are referred to as "children in care" (NSPCC, 2014).

According to the research statistics presented by NSPCC, there are 90,000 children in care at any one time in the United Kingdom. Many of these children have suffered a form of abuse and neglect, and 45 per cent have been diagnosed with mental health conditions (McAuley and Davis, 2009). This makes them more vulnerable in society, hence the reasons for them to be placed in the care system. Children in care settings tend to have less optimal outcomes than the wider population in regard to educational achievement, homelessness, and mental health. All these outcomes sometimes make it difficult for practitioners and professionals to determine the extent to which these outcomes were caused by the child's or young person's experiences prior to them coming into care, rather than what they experienced when in care.

It is wrong to assume that all children in care are kept safe and protected, as many children and young people are at risk of abuse and neglect from their carers, support workers, other young people, and the general population, who sees them as a target due to their vulnerability and disabilities. Bell's 2012 guide to participatory practice explores the foundation of children's participation in decisions that affect them. It identifies the values, skills, and knowledge practitioners and professionals need to implement effective practices to engage children and young people. According to the Children Act 1989, it aims to focus on the involvement of children and young people in different aspects of decision-making. Follow-up legislation and guidance documents continue to encourage children's right to participate, mainly focusing on organisational policy and change. This can be seen in the development of Every Child Matters (Department for Education and Skills, or DFES, 2004), an initiative which has key components of five outcomes to ensure the participation of children in decision-making. These outcomes are as follows: be healthy, stay safe, enjoy, achieve, make a positive contribution, and achieve economic well-being. The policies of Every Child Matters work in conjunction with the Children Act 2004, which contains important legislation that governs children's rights to participation in decision-making.

In terms of the discussion above, it is important that the children's rights are always considered and acknowledged. This is also emphasised by Harding (1997), who used the terms "children's rights" and "child liberation" in a perspective that emphasises the importance of the child's own viewpoint and wishes, seeing the child as a separate entity with rights to autonomy and freedom, rather like adults. Furthermore, she argued that "the strength of children, and their similarity to adults, is emphasised, rather than their vulnerability" (Harding, 1997).

Article 12 of the (UNCRC) clearly agrees with this perspective on children's rights. This article summarises the importance of respecting the views of the child and states that when adults are making decisions that affect children, these children and young people have the right to say what they think should happen, and their opinions should be taken into account. This article encourages adults to listen to children's opinions and involve them in the decision-making process. On the other hand, this article does not overlook the rights of parents to express and share their own views on matters affecting their children, but it recognises factors that could affect a child's ability to make their own decisions. For example, a child who suffers from mental health or learning difficulty, or a child who is highly disabled and nonverbal—that is, lacking the means or ability to communicate their views or wishes effectively—may have their decision-making rights deferred to their legal guardian.

Another article listed under the UNCRC promoting the rights

of children is Article 3 (Best Interests of the Child). It considers the best interest of the child the main priority when making important decisions that may affect them. Practitioners and professionals should at all times do what is in the best interest of the child to meet their specific needs, striving to meet the five outcomes of Every Child Matters, in accordance to the "Working Together to Safeguard Children" (2013) guidance document. This article particularly applies to budget, policy, and law makers.

Furthermore, the Child's Rights Convention (CRC) covers the whole range of human rights of children, referred to as the Four Ps. These are as follows: provision, protection, prevention, and participation. Provision, according to Article 27 of the UNCRC, states that "children have the right to a standard of living that is good enough to meet the physical and mental needs" (UNICEF, 2014). This does not exclude CLA. All children have the right to be treated fairly and given the right resources to develop. The protection of children is also mentioned in Article 19, which states that children have the right to be protected from being hurt and mistreated, both physically and mentally. This article takes the child's best interests into consideration.

One of the most important issues the convention covers is prevention. According to a famous saying, "Prevention is better than cure." For example, preventing illness is better and cheaper than healing it. This applies to other issues as well. For example, it is cheaper to grant primary education to every child than to invest in educating adults so they can adapt to the challenges of a modern economy. Furthermore, prevention not only is the responsibility of the government but requires the involvement of society in general. The most controversial of the Ps is participation, as mentioned in Article 12. It states that all children's rights must be respected, and the level of a child's participation in decisions must be appropriate to the child's level of maturity and ability to form their own opinions and views.

Theoretical Perspective: Social Model of Disability

Disability is defined as a state of having a physical or mental impairment, where the impairment places a long-term limitation on a person's physical, mental, or sensory function (Scope, 2014). The social model is one of the three types of model that exist, the others being the medical (or individual) model and the rights model. In the social model, disability is constructed by society rather than being the "fault" of the individual. In the medical model, people are disabled by their impairments or differences (Conradie and Golding, 2013). For example, a young person with a learning disability wants to live independently in their own home but is uncertain of how to pay their bills. In regard to the social model, that young person would be supported with their day-to-day living and paying their bills. On the other hand, under the medical model, that young person might be expected to live in a residential home with other young people.

Using the social model of disability means that an individual with a disability is seen primarily as a person and the impairment is seen on secondary terms. As a result, this research is informed by a poststructuralist theoretical perspective.

CHAPTER 2

PARTICIPATION

Marsh and Fisher (1992) were quoted as saying, "Users can play a key role in informing the development of policy and practice … but that belief in the value of partnership contrasts with the low recognition of users' views. Staff may resist change towards participation, openness and information because they 'do this already'" (Bell, 2012).

The importance of the above quote cannot be overstated, especially in practice issues when talking about participation. Participation is not, and should not be, about ticking the boxes or making up statistical information; it is about the production of a visible, tangible change. Resistance to change opposes effective participation. Effective participation embraces openness and encourages the voice of all participants to be heard, thereby producing a change that informs the development of policy and practice for the better.

What is participation? Bell (2012) quoted Kirby et al. (2003) as describing participation as a multi-layered concept which embraces notions of both process and outcome. The United Nations Committee on the Rights of the Child 2012, Article 12, also strongly emphasises the importance of process and outcome as aspects of participation, and it describes how the term has evolved and is now widely used to describe ongoing processes, including information sharing and communication between children and adults (professionals and practitioners). Another definition of participation is used to describe different types and levels of involvement, listing activities that take place in different ways. This list consists of different types of engagement, such as representation, consultation, and advocacy in different situations. As participation aims to involve service users in the decision-making of all aspects of their lives, it is a key social skill that all professionals and practitioners should have to enable all young people and children participate actively in the processes.

Participation engages children and makes them feel part of a participatory process. Participatory action process (PAP) is a methodology whereby the cared for and the carer both discover and make meanings together. It is a process whereby the carer engages the cared for. It is in the process of engagement that the needs of the cared for are discovered and understood. The discovery and understanding of those needs will dictate the specific support needed. This process is in contrast to the mainstream general guidelines set out for all, in which specific needs are not met or ignored. In light of this, children's voices must be heard through participation when designing a care package or support plan to protect the emotional well-being of children and young people. For children's voices to be heard, the importance of participation cannot be overemphasised.

Participation can take place in different levels and circumstances; a lot of it is based on child protection cases and reviews, and it involves promoting organisational change at local, regional, national, and international levels. This type of participation shows a clear level of power-sharing between children and adults with regards to the nature and context of the situation. On the other hand, when a case of decision-making includes organisational change, the effectiveness of participation depends upon the skills of the practitioners supporting the change.

Participation also aims to achieve different outcomes for different reasons. It could be for personal empowerment in decision-making or vast organisational changes. For CLA, it is commonly believed that they are not properly engaged in the decision-making process. Bell (2012) quoted Sinclair, Wilson, and Gibbs (2004) as saying, "The frequency and nature of the participation will vary widely, as will children and young people involved." This quote is particularly relevant for CLA because there are verbal and nonverbal CLA in care settings. For verbal CLA, it is known to be easier to communicate with them and help them get their views across, as they possess at least limited communication. However, it is a greater challenge to communicate with nonverbal children, as they have difficulty expressing themselves verbally and understanding what is being communicated to them.

Communication is a key component of participation of CLA, especially nonverbal CLA, in decision-making. In their case, advocacy may be required whereby practitioners need to familiarize themselves with nonverbal communication systems and know how to contact suitable interpreters or facilitators, or human aids to communication (HACs). "Advocacy in all its forms seeks to ensure that people are able to speak out to express their views and defend their rights" (Mind, 2013). In this perspective, "children are seen as subject rather than object of others' actions and choices, as actors with the ability to define their situations and arrive at independent decisions" (Harding, 1997). This emphasises the fact that looked-after children should be seen as rational beings (that is, we should have faith in them), rather than see them on the basis of their disabilities. In contrast to the assertion of Harding (1997) that children should be seen as a separate entity with rights to autonomy and freedom, rather like adults, Bell (2012) argued that when determining children's competence in taking part in decision-making, three key factors should be considered: age, ability, and culture. For example, when talking about age, maturity should play a key, role but this argument can be challenged in the case of a looked-after child with severe learning difficulties who finds it difficult to communicate. A child's ability to communicate their views does not depend solely on age. Communication depends on level of ability, behavioural difficulties, and the emotional abuse an eighteen-year-old might have suffered, and this is not always considered or identified when putting a care plan or support plan in place to meet the needs of that child or young person. On the other hand, a seven-year-old without learning difficulties might be able to communicate his or her views better. Consequently, the ability to communicate, it can be argued, is tied not only to age but to disability. Culture also plays a significant role in the participation of decision-making. Lack of understanding and awareness of differing cultural beliefs could affect the engagement of children in decision-making.

Furthermore, participation allows for empowerment. It encourages these children to express themselves for their voices to be heard. Participation which leads to empowerment also makes children believe that they and their views are respected. Braye and Preston-Shoot (1995) define empowerment as "the process of taking control of one's own life, of moving from a position of vulnerability or lacking power toward a position of enhanced power" (Bell, 2012). However, this becomes an area of challenge in practice for children with severe learning disabilities, as decisions are usually made on their behalf.

The participation of children and young people in decisions that affect their lives is a central platform of current government policy. Thirty years ago, the Children Act 1975 placed a duty on local authorities "to ascertain as far as is practicable the wishes and feelings of the child and give due consideration to them, having regard to his/her age and understanding" (Stein, 2009). Article 23 (Children with Disabilities) of the UNCRC states, "Children who have any kind of disability have the right to special care and support, as well as all rights in the convention, so that they can live full and independent lives" (UNICEF, 2014).

It is vital that children and young people with any form of disability feel like they are part of something; their input is extremely beneficial throughout the process. It is unlikely that a child or young person who has learning difficulties or is nonverbal would be able to express his or her views and be initiated into the participatory process, but there are ways around this problem, namely, advocacy participation.

Advocacy is a process which helps an individual speak up for themselves and access information on their rights and entitlement. It is also a process to stop, start, or change something (Welsh Government, 2009). Advocacy plays a key role in allowing children and young people to participate in safeguarding and promoting their own rights in relation to the UNCRC. The local authorities must ensure that all children, young people, and their families are provided with support and informed access to services, both local and national, in relation to children's welfare and protection. All information should be made clear and available in the preferred family language. An independent advocate should be used at all times and should provide confidential information, advice, support, and good representation should the need arise.

The case for an independent advocate is paramount in the advocacy process, as family members and friends are likely perpetrators of domestic and child abuse, thus causing conflicts of interests (HM Government, 2006). An example is an account by Chong (2006) of a 14-year-old Chinese boy named Tony. Tony's school informed children's services about a disclosure Tony made: that his father forced him to work in the family's takeaway shop and also threatened him with a knife. Tony lived with his parents, two brothers, and grandmother in the takeaway shop. Only his father spoke English. A social worker got involved in the case. His father was resentful towards the social worker, and the family saw the social worker as a "figure of authority". When the social worker visited the home, the family refused to co-operate, and Tony denied any disclosure. This made it difficult for the social worker to involve him in any participatory process and decision-making. This case demonstrated the need for independent advocacy in cases of safeguarding children.

Culture also plays a major role when considering safeguarding children. Children from different cultures are likely to be subjected to abuse and significant harm because of cultural norms and beliefs. These cultural factors include language barriers, differing lifestyles, and religious beliefs. Specifically, language barriers have a major impact on communication concerning the participation of children and young people in decisions that affect them. Communication can be misinterpreted because the context is not understood.

It is harder when the child or young person cannot communicate in English or is nonverbal. This makes it more difficult for that child to communicate and participate in any decision-making; hence, an advocate must effectively represent that child or young person, putting the best interests of the child at the forefront of all decision-making. Also, it is the responsibility of all practitioners working with children to ensure that the views of children are heard. Irrespective of a child's age or ability to communicate their feelings, practitioners should facilitate different methods to achieve their aims (e.g., through pictures, drawings, social stories, symbols, and creativity). Practitioners must interpret exactly what the child has communicated to them, not what they think has been communicated. For example, they might include a clear and precise drawing of what has been communicated by a child. When it comes to decision-making, the child's view is not always considered, but an interpretation by the adult is considered instead. All practitioners must be trained in communicating with children or young people who are nonverbal or lack understanding. The importance of training was highlighted in a study carried out by Franklin and Sloper in 2009, in which practitioners used a technique to get deaf children to express their views. The children were asked to draw a "map/ diagram of all the people that have supported them when they were going through sadness." They wrote the questions for their service providers on brightly coloured pieces of paper, and then the children were helped to write down their answers (Bell, 2009). This illustrates that children's views can still be heard despite inherent disabilities.

Nonverbal communication can be described as a form of bodily communication that ranges from different types of nonverbal signals, such as facial expression, nonverbal vocalisations, posture, bodily contact, and gestures (Hartley, 1993).

The NSPCC (2005) stressed the responsibility of practitioners to safeguard children and young people with learning disabilities and provide them with relevant information, advice, and support. Practitioners are also responsible for giving them a voice which enables them to take charge of their lives. With that said, Chand (2005) stated, "It is not enough to simply have an interpreter who can speak the appropriate language: the concepts associated with child maltreatment and neglect are very different from those concerning welfare benefits. ... Interpreters who are competent in the latter might find themselves at a loss when trying to interpret terms around child abuse" (Bell, 2012).

This demonstrates the need to develop policies and guidelines that are specific to issues of safeguarding children looked after (CLA) without relying on the general or uniform guidelines for all welfare cases. In addition to all factors mentioned above, it is possible to prevent the risk of child abuse and neglect if and when we implement effective strategies based on the New Working Together to Safeguard Children (2013) guidelines, the Children Act (1989 and 2004) and the Quality

Matters policy. The Children Act 1989 emphasises safeguarding and promoting the welfare of children in its definition—to protect children from maltreatment and prevent impairment of children's health or development, according to the Every Child Matters "Five Outcomes" document (GOV, 2013).

In the next chapter, will look in more detail at the protection of children looked after.

CHAPTER 3

PROTECTION

The protection of children from harm has been of existence in the Children Act 1989 legislation for over twenty decades. This act can be seen as the first substantial law that established major child protection structures and principles still being implemented today.

Article 2 of the Human Rights Act (1998) states that everyone has "the right to life". Every child death where the public authorities were aware of a real and immediate risk to the child and failed to act could be claimed to be a breach of this article (HRA, 1998).

Looking at history, child protection has been and is still a recurring issue in welfare services. Take, for example, as reported by Professor Nigel Parton in *Child Abuse Review* in July 2003, the tragic death of 7-year-old Maria Colwell in 1973. Maria had been in the care of the local authorities in Brighton from a tender age before she went to live with her biological mother and stepfather. Maria was described by her foster parents as a happy little girl. At the time of her death, at the hands of her stepfather, who at the time was the subject of a supervision order with his biological children, there were concerns about his ill-treatment of Maria. Furthermore, various people, including teachers and neighbours, expressed their concerns to social services. The home was visited by a number of professionals, and yet nothing was done.

Maria died of severe internal injuries and brain damage. Maria's death became a public concern and received much media attention, leading to the Colwell inquiry report in 1974.

"According to Parton and Thomas, 1983, the public inquiry into the death of Maria Colwell can be seen as a watershed in the contemporary history of social work, particularly in social services department. Before this, social work practice was seen primarily as private activities carried out between clients and professionals, the latter optimistically feeling their skills and techniques could tackle, even solve many social problems" (Frost and Parton, 2009).

In addition to the inquiry reports in 1974 and 1985, there were twenty-nine further inquiries into the deaths of children as a result of abuse. The report of the Committee of Inquiry into the Care and Supervision Provided in Relation to Maria Colwell, chaired by Thomas Gilbert Fisher, identified three main contributory factors: "the lack of communication between the agencies who were aware of her vulnerable situation, inadequate training for social workers assigned to 'at-risk' children and changes in the make-up of society" (Children Webmag, 2009).

All children and young people have the right to protection in all aspects of their lives. Over the years, there major serious case reviews and inquiries have led to child deaths in the UK. February 2000 saw the death of Victoria Climbie, a young child who died with 128 separate injuries on her body after months of abuse by her aunt and boyfriend. Despite Victoria coming into contact with professionals, such as social workers, health visitors, and the police, none of them could prevent the abuse which led to her death. It was clear that Victoria was being abused. She had been admitted to hospital twice, and not a single practitioner felt she was at significant risk of harm and neglect. As a result of Victoria's death, the government published a green paper entitled, "Every Child Matters", which was incorporated in the Children Act 2004 with the aim of formulating changes and eliminating child-protection registers in favour of child-protection plans. The goal was to create an integrated children's computer system (ICS) to ensure information was shared accordingly and appropriately. This goes to show that lack of information sharing increases the risk of significant harm to a child or young person and makes it more difficult to safeguard and promote the welfare of children (Community Care, 2014).

Another case is that of Baby P, or Peter Connelly, in 2008. Peter was a 17-month-old toddler who died after suffering serious internal and external injuries over nine months. Despite being seen by a multitude of professionals and being the focus of a child-protection plan, practitioners were not even aware that this toddler's mother had a boyfriend, who, along with a friend, was responsible for Peter's death.

It is extremely disturbing that both Victoria and Baby P died in Haringey, under the same local authority. As a result, Working Together to Safeguard Children's guidance was put forward alongside the ICS to ensure that relevant and essential information is always shared among all professionals and practitioners working with children and young people. This ensures their safety and needs are met in accordance with the legislation. Baby P was under the umbrella of a "child in need" suffering from significant harm. "If it is decided that the child is in need of further support from social services, they are officially designated a child in need; as defined by section 17 of the Children Act 1989" (NSPCC, 2014).

Clearly, there is a gap between policy and practice, as most practitioners and professionals working with children and young people, with or without a disability, are unprofessional and unreliable when it comes to sharing information. Evidence shows that many children have suffered forms of abuse and been subjected to significant harm due to lack of information-sharing. Information-sharing is important as it allows the delivery of services to be effective and coordinated based on the needs of the individual. The need for information-sharing guidance is essential, as many practitioners know the importance of information-sharing yet are sometimes hesitant or uncertain about when it is lawful to share. It was asserted that practitioners struggle with information-sharing in cases that involve early intervention and prevention work, because the decisions made are not clear in certain safeguarding or child-protection situations (HM Government, 2008).

In addition, it is vital that information shared amongst professionals remain confidential, but only until the child is at risk of suffering significant harm or abuse. A child or young person who is unable to communicate to practitioners for reasons such as disability, age, or fear of speaking out is likely at risk of suffering some form of abuse and in danger of significant harm. This is commonly found in children with disabilities or learning difficulties. In this case, it is useful to involve an independent advocate in matters affecting them. As a practitioner, if you have concerns about a child or young person being at risk of significant harm, you should always consider referring your concerns to children's social care, the police, and the Local Safeguarding Children Board (LSCB). Practitioners should make sure they have relevant facts and evidenced information when making a referral or disclosure and avoid being presumptuous, as things might not be the way they seem.

Cleaver and Walker (2004) state that the process of protecting a child or young person is outlined in the Working Together guidance document 2006, which bears relevance to the Assessment Framework and all protocols under section 47 of the Children Act 1989. Local authorities must investigate where there is a reason to believe that a child is suffering or is likely to suffer significant harm (Kirton, 2008). It is worthy to note that most of the time, arrivals of new referrals are made to social services by other professionals, such as health visitors, teachers, family workers, the police, and in most cases the family members but never the children. As a result, we might logically ask why children are not coming forward to make disclosures that will ensure their protection. Likely, the children are either too scared to speak out, fearing further abuse, or afraid of stigmatization. The latter case is clearly evident, as Kirton (2008) states, "The contrast between children's extensive uptake of Childline's anonymous and confidential service and the very low level of self-referral to welfare agencies is striking."

Consequently, we must develop processes that address the fears and concerns of children. This will ensure that children can make disclosures or referrals in a comfortable, non-threatening environment without fear of being at risk of further harm or stigmatisation. The best interest of the child is once again paramount in the protection of children and young people. According to UNCRC, in its convention on the rights of the child, "All children have the right to be protected from abuse or exploitation" (Save the Children, 2014). To improve protection for children looked after (CLA) and disabled children, we must have a clear aim of child protection and a definition of good practice.

In a CLA setting, there should always be an awareness of the risk of abuse and openness to allow room for criticism and for improvement and progression to take place. When considering what's best for the child or young person, we must tailor a plan to the child's individual needs. Not only does such an environment cater to children that are homeless or have family difficulties, but it also helps children with severe disabilities and challenging behaviours. When dealing with such vulnerable children (CLA), many factors have to be considered, and practitioners should promote these children's rights and privacy. They should take into account their cultural beliefs, ethnicity, age, religion, abilities, and disabilities. Most of all, that child should be seen as an individual and should be treated equally, with dignity and respect. Concerning their rights, each child should have a right to privacy, and their rights should be outlined in guidelines for practitioners to implement good working practice—particularly in cases of intimate care when working with children of the opposite sex or when addressing difficult or challenging behaviour and consent to treatment. Article 16 of the UNCRC, in its right-to-privacy section, states that "children have a right to privacy and the law should protect them from attacks against their way of life, their good name, their families and their homes" (UNICEF, 2014).

A report by Utting (1997) showed that children and young people with disabilities and challenging behaviour made suggestions as to how they wished to be cared for, especially concerning the safety of their own residential care settings. These children expressed their views of what services they wanted in these settings. For example, their lists mentioned the kind of staff they desired and the attributes these individuals should have, such as good character, sense of humour, willingness to work, understanding of children, unaggressive behaviour towards children. They wanted staff who have been scrutinized, give children a choice of services and support, make their experiences in care and all aspects positive and rewarding, and are protective of children. They also expressed an interest in security cameras, security alarms, and security guards (Utting, 1997).

In light of the above, it is imperative that in protecting children looked after, their views are sought and considered when making decisions relating to them. It is in seeking their views that we can truly say we are working together to safeguard and protect children and young people.

CHAPTER 4

PREVENTION

"Article 19 (Protection from all forms of violence) states that, "Children have the right to be protected from being hurt and mistreated, physically or mentally. Government should ensure that children are properly cared for and protect them from violence, abuse and neglect by their parents or anyone else who looks after them" (UNICEF, 2014).

Evidence shows that institutional care can cause serious harm to children. The quality of care in these settings compared to the standards of services provided is average, subjecting these children and young people to abuse and harm. In a report titled, "Keeping Children Out of Harmful Institutions", written by Corinna Csaky, the United Nations estimated that 8 million children around the world live in care institutions, and during the early twentieth century, it was found that harm can be caused to children by institutional care, exposing a historical issue that had been in practice for quite some time. Furthermore, it showed that many children in institutional care, especially under the age of 3, suffer abuse and neglect that could affect their development permanently. Such children should be placed in a family setting, because long-term residence in such institutions can have a lasting and negative impact on the lives of these vulnerable children (Save the Children, 2009).

Most of the children who have been put in care have parents but are placed in care for different reasons. Some of the reasons are linked to the social exclusion experienced by vulnerable families, which prevents such families from gaining access to certain services, such as welfare assistance, employment, and housing. Furthermore, some parents are simply impoverished, struggling daily to provide basic needs like food, clothing, and shelter for their families. Sometimes, some families place their children in care as they feel it is the only way for their children to gain access to good education, food, and other benefits. There are huge concerns around the standard and quality of care that result in various types of abuse CLA are subjected to. Stein (2009), in his book *Quality Matters,* elaborates on the Quality Protects Programme in children's services. He believes practitioners should put themselves in the shoes of parents and ask the question: If that were my child, would the quality of services be of a reasonable standard, and would it be good enough for me? Also, he talks about the main aim of improving outcomes for children and young people who are in need, in particular, CLA.

Research shows there are poor educational and career outcomes for many children and young people leaving care. Statistics show that more than 75 per cent of care leavers have no qualifications or achievements, and over half of young people leaving care aged 16 or above are unemployed. There has been a significant amount of abuse in children's homes as a result of the low quality of care. The blame here must be placed on the doorstep of lack of funding. However, funding was put aside to achieve the outcomes outlined in the Quality Protects Programme, which the Department of Health set up in September 1998.

Abuse of CLA and children with disabilities is a recurring and ongoing issue. For example, in a recent review research study carried out by Stalker and McArthur, between the year 1996 and 2009, using a five-stage method for scoping studies, showed that many children with disabilities are significantly more likely to experience abuse than those without a disability. At greatest risk are children with a particular impairment. Factors such as age, gender, and sociocultural interaction have a high degree of incidence among abused children without disabilities. According to Stalker and McArthur (2012), "In Britain it appears that some therapeutic services and criminal justice system often fail to take into account the needs of children with disabilities and their heightened vulnerability and little is known of what happens to children with disabilities and how well safeguarding services address their needs." In addition, it seems that fewer studies have pursued the interpretations of children who have experienced abuse or safeguarding issues. There is clearly an underlying problem at the level of both policy and practice when it comes to promoting the rights and protection of children.

A comparative analysis between studies carried out in the UK and other countries—research done by Sullivan and Knutson (2000) in America—found clear and reliable facts that children with disabilities suffer a higher risk of abuse than their non-disabled peers. They conducted research using a community-based population, with children ranging from age 0 to 21 who enrolled in education programmes between 1994 and 1995 to identify children with impairments and those without. Among those without disabilities, the rate of abuse was 9 percent. On the other hand, among children with disabilities, was the rate was 31 per cent, showing that children with impairments were three to four times more likely to suffer a form of abuse or maltreatment compared with those without impairment. Other studies were carried out in different countries to identify the increasing risk of abuse among children with disabilities. For example, in Norway, Kvam (2004) surveyed 302 deaf adults who were on the Norwegian Deaf Register and found out that 134 of them had been victims of unwanted sexual abuse during their childhood. In Sweden, according to Stalker and McArthur (2012), Jemta et al. (2008) interviewed sixty-nine 13- to 18-year-olds with mobility impairments about their sexual experiences, and a small number of young people (five) reported to have been sexually abused. This study, amongst others, clearly shows that there is an increased risk of abuse suffered by children with disabilities.

In the UK, it was evidenced that there was limited information regarding the prevalence of abuse among children with disabilities. According to Stalker and McArthur (2012), Balogh et al. (2001) carried out an investigation on forty-three patients from a child and adolescent psychiatric unit. Twenty-one of these children had been sexually abused. On the other hand, Morris (1999) reported that children with disabilities from a local authority comprised only 2 per cent of the total age range of 0 to 17, and yet 10 per cent of these were on the child protection register. Another research was carried out by Cooke and Standen (2002), which found that the quality of information sharing in the UK was substandard. In Britain, a survey was carried out on seventy-three Area Child Protection Committees (ACPCs); 50 per cent of these committees claimed to have recorded an occurrence of impairment of children placed on child-protection registers, and only ten ACPCs could actually give a number. In addition to the above, these children were placed on the child protection register for sexual abuse. Concerning sexual abuse, Parton and Wattam (1999) quoted Kilkess (1989) as saying, "'The more intrusive policing' investigative child protection response has retained its legitimacy despite the tendency to review children's needs on a less formal preventative level in relation to other forms of maltreatment." However, sexual abuse should not be treated as the major for the only form of abuse. Practitioners and professionals should always consider other forms of abuse and maltreatment as equally important and having nearly the same outcome.

Spencer et al. (2005) "established in reviewing the case of almost 120,000 children born between the year 1983 and 2001 in West Sussex that children with a form of disability 'seemed to be' at increased risk of registration for abuse and neglect, although this is wide-ranging in relation to those with a disability." Furthermore, information about disability status was incorporated in the Scottish Government Child Protection Statistics for the first time in the year 2008-2009. It was evidenced that 7 per cent of children on child-protection registers had a form of disability. On the hand, 23 per cent of children on the register had an unknown disability status, and no other comparable data was composed in England, Wales, or Northern Ireland (Scottish Government, 2009). There is likely extensive evidence to propose that the abuse of children with disabilities is underreported. In light of this assertion, we can argue that the abuse of children is not being effectively prevented because effective working policy and guidelines addressing the prevention of abuse of children looked after cannot be developed without adequate information. Accurate statistical data and information for research work on abuse of CLA will build a platform to recognize flaws and errors. These flaws and errors can then be corrected in further research to develop policy guidelines to address current and developing issues concerning the abuse of children. As the popular saying goes, "Prevention is better than cure, because cure is not certain."

CHAPTER 5

PROVISION

In terms of provision, the "best interest of the child" should be at the forefront of all decision-making, in addition to following the guidelines enshrined in the Every Child Matters "Five Outcomes" document. Save the Children believe that a family-based care setting should be the first option for children requiring alternative care (Save the Children, 2009). In such settings, a number of key factors should be considered by lawmakers and practitioners to acknowledge the vulnerability of disabled children most likely to suffer abuse. In an interview carried out by Helen Westcott with adults who had suffered some form of abuse as children, she recognised factors as "physical and social isolation, lack of choice, lack of physical and psychological resources to defend oneself, physical immobility and the ability to switch off one's body at will (The latter because of frequent intrusive behaviour by professionals and adults)" (Utting, 1997). For children with complex disabilities, the provision of residential care setting is mostly considered to be in the best interest of that individual and specifically for that individual to feel safe, respected, and cared for. Article 23 of the UNCRC, addressing the rights for children with disabilities, states, "Children who have any kind of disability have the right to special care and support, as well as all rights in the Convention, so they can live full and independent lives" (UNICEF, 2014).

The provision for CLA and children in need is highly important and should be followed in line with the Ofsted regulations and guidelines. In one of the publications by Ofsted prioritising the experiences of children who need help, protection, and care were prioritised in a single framework that was put together with the aim of inspecting the services provided by the local authority to vulnerable children, such as CLA. This inspection was conducted over a period of three years and came into effect in November 2013, specifically for CLA and care leavers. The inspections were carried out under section 136 of the Education and Inspections Act 2006, focusing on the effectiveness of local authority services and arrangements to help and protect children, monitor the experiences they have both in and out of care, and ensure they live in safe and resourceful environments, one that encourages them to progress and achieve in relation to the Working Together to Safeguard Children and Young People document (Ofsted, 2014). In addition to this inspection, a review of the efficiency of the Local Safeguarding Children Board would be conducted in accordance with section 15(A) of the Children Act 2004 in its duties to provide services for children and young people, via the local authority.

As mentioned above, concerning physical, sexual, and emotional abuse and neglect, children looked after are most vulnerable to such experiences. It is not only the duty of practitioners but also the local authority as a whole to make sure all children and young people placed under their care are looked after and protected from harm and neglect at all times. According to the Working Together to Safeguard Children document, the local authority has the duty to provide adequate food, clothing, and shelter, including when children and young people are excluded from home or abandoned. Lack of provision translates to "neglect". The term "neglect" is defined as, "the persistent failure to meet a child's basic physical and/or psychological needs, and its likeliness to result to potential serious impairments of the child's health or development" (HM Government, 2006).

The local authority has responsibility for safeguarding and promoting the welfare of children who are excluded from school or suffer any form of impairment. CLA and young people should have the same opportunities as other children and young people, including the five outcomes outlined in Every Child Matters and enshrined in the Children Act 1989 and 2004 legislation documents. According to the National Institute for Health and Care Excellence (NICE), it was found that, in March 2012, there were 67,050 looked-after children and young people in England. Of these, 75 per cent were placed in foster care, while 12 per cent were in residential settings, including residential schools and secure units (NICE, 2014). However, according to NICE 2014, 60 per cent of CLA in England suffer from emotional and mental difficulties, and a high number are likely to experience poor health, educational problems, and social problems after they have left care. This means that over 50 per cent of children looked after and young people suffer lack of provision or different forms of abuse. The staggering number of children who suffer is alarming, especially for children looked after. It was also found that in the beginning of the year up to April 2012, the number of children who, due to any form of abuse or neglect, ended in care settings, averaged 62 per cent (NICE, 2014).

Article 28 of the United Nations Conventions on the Rights of the Child (UNCRC), in its Rights to Education, states, "All children have the right to a primary education; the convention places a high value on education and states that all young people should be encouraged to reach the highest level of education of which they are capable" (UNICEF, 2014).

All children and young people should have a right to good education and a right to the outcomes stated in the Every Child Matters policy document. These outcomes are as follows: be healthy, stay safe, enjoy and achieve, make a positive contribution, and achieve economic well-being. All practitioners should work towards supporting CLA to achieve their full potential in their educational progression.

The legislative provisions of the Department for Children, Schools and Families (DCSF) state that the local authority must safeguard and promote the welfare of CLA and, in particular, a duty to promote the child's educational achievement. It also places a duty on the local authority to safeguard and promote the welfare of children looked after, and in particular, the child's educational achievement. This duty was placed on the local authority because it was found that though some children looked after do well, "the educational achievement of children looked after as a group remains unacceptably low" (DCSF, 2010).

In the provision of health services to CLA and all young people, the National Service Framework for Children, Young People and Maternity Services (NSF) set out a ten-year programme for improving the quality of services for children, young people, and pregnant women. Section 11 of the Children Act 2004 places a duty on strategic health authorities, designated special hospitals, primary care trusts, NHS trusts, and NHS foundation trusts. All these must ensure that, in the provision of their services, they safeguard and promote the welfare of children (HM Government, 2013). The duty placed on these health authorities is extremely important in the provision of care, especially to CLA, because a greater number of CLA have varying forms of disabilities. Practitioners should liaise closely with other agencies to recognise and understand the specific needs of CLA to provide effective and adequate health services and resources.

In summary, Article 24 of the UNCRC relating to health and

health services states, "Children have the right to good quality health care – the best health care possible – to safe drinking water, nutritious food, a clean and safe environment and information to help them stay healthy" (UNICEF, 2014). As a result, all practitioners and professionals must work together to provide the basic needs of every child looked after to ensure that they have a safe and stable environment, prioritising the best interest of the child. This will ensure a healthy emotional and physical well-being.

CONCLUSION

"Article 20 of the UNCRC (children deprived of family environment) states that, 'Children who cannot be looked after by their own family have a right to special care and must be looked after properly by people who respect their ethnic group, religion, culture and language'" (UNICEF, 2014).

In conclusion, as stated above, CLAs are vulnerable to various forms of abuse. Hence, it is necessary to ensure that all professionals and practitioners work together in effecting Article 20 of the UNCRC (stated above), because it will be double jeopardy for these children if they are not given another chance to maximise all aspects of their growth in a stable environment close to a family setting. This is because CLAs, for whatever reasons, have already been displaced from their homes or have not their families have otherwise been unable to look after them. As a result, they need consistent and reassuring care to ensure that their physical, emotional, and psychological well-being is not harmed further.

As illustrated above, operating the four Ps model is paramount and relevant in achieving the five outcomes of Every Child Matters and in creating a safe and healthy environment for CLA. Each of the P's (participation, protection, prevention, and provision) is of equal relevance, and their importance cannot be overemphasised in ensuring that CLA are provided with the duty of care owed to them. Without participation, the CLA's "voice" is drowned and not heard. Without protection, their lives are disrupted from following their natural course and are exposed to lifelong pain. Without prevention, we are not getting it right the first time. And without provision, we are certainly failing them, and the results will certainly be disastrous.

Every child is a potential future human capital of every nation. If children, whether CLA or otherwise, are deprived of their due care and support, then we as a nation are depriving ourselves of what could be. Hence, we must see every child for who he or she is and see impairment for what it is. As aptly put by (Thomas, 2004), "Disability is social exclusion on the grounds of impairment, impairment does not cause disability, certainly not, but it is the raw material upon which disability works." This goes to show that the social model sees an individual first and sees the impairment second (medical model). The social model is relevant to the four P's (participation, protection, prevention, and provision) because it allows the individual to take a primary position in the scheme of things, and the disability takes a secondary position. This position helps foster equality, because every child, whether children looked after or otherwise, is seen as equals and treated the same way. The individual is not seen as lacking, but the disability is seen in its own context and accommodated. As a result, children looked after can fully participate in issues that concern them, enabling the prevention of stereotypical attitudes toward them, thereby protecting them from all forms of abuse (whether physical or emotional); this ensures that their rights are met in the provision of adequate care for them.

REFERENCES

Anon., n.d. *Every Child Matters Information.* [Online]

Available at: ncvys.org.uk

Children Webmag, 2011. *The Maria Colwell Report: Chaired by T.G Field-Fisher.* [Online] Available at: at: http://www.childrenwebmag.com/articles/key-child-care-texts/the-maria-colwell-reportchaired-by-tg-field-fisher

Community Care, 2005. *Child Protection.* [Online]

Available at: http://www.communitycare.co.uk/2005/03/15/child-protection-3/#U3ixgcu9KSM

Conradie, L. & Golding, T., 2013. *The Short Guide to Working with children and young people.* Bristol: The Policy Press.

Cooper, M., Hooper, C. & Thompson, M., 2005. *Child and Adolescent Mental Health.* New York: Hodder Arnold.

DCSF, 2010. *Looking after Children: Legislation and National Guidance.* [Online]

Available at: ttp://www.commissioningsupport.org.uk/resource-bank/children-and-families/lac-policy-and-guidance.html

Department Of Health, 1998. *Caring for Children Away From Home.* Chichester, New York, Weinheim, Brisbane, Singapore & Toronto: John Wiley & Son Ltd.

European Agency, 2014. *European Agency for Special Needs and Inclusive Education.* [Online]

Available at: http://www.european-agency.org/about-us/contacts

Frost, N. & Parton, N., 2009. *Understanding Children's Social Care.* London: Sage Publications.

Glaser, D. & Prior, V., 1997. Is the child protection applicable to emotional abuse?. *Child Abuse Review,* Volume 6, pp. 315-329.

Harding, L. F., 1991. *Perspectives in Child Care Policy.* 2nd ed. Harlow: Pearson Education.

Hartley, P., 1999. *Interpersonal Communication.* London & New York: Routledge.

HM Government, 20018. *Information Sharing Pocket Guide.* [Online] Available at: http://www.plymouth.gov.uk/information_sharing_pocked_guide.pdf

HM Government, 2006. *Working Together to Safeguard Children.* London: TSO.

HM Government, 2008. *Information Sharing Guidance for practitioners and managers.* [Online] Available at: http://www.everychildmatters.gov.uk/informationsharing

HM Government, 2013. *Working Together Safeguard Children: A guide to inter-agency working to safeguard and promote the welfare of children.* [Online] Available at: http://www.tsoshop.co.uk/bookstore.asp

Howe, D., 2005. *Child Abuse and Neglect: Attachment, Development and Intervention.* s.l.: Palgrave Macmillan.

Kirton, D., 2008. Looked After Children - The State as Parent. *Child Social Work Policy & Practice,* pp. 104-128.

Kirton, D., 2008. Safeguarding Children: Contemporary Policy and Pratice. *Child Social Work Policy & Practice,* pp. 63-80.

Mason, J. & Fattore, T., 2005. *Children Take Seriously.* London: Jessica Kingsley Publishers Limited.

McAuley, C. & Davis, T., 2009. Emotional Well-being and mental health of looked after children in England. *Child & Family Social Work*, Volume 14, pp. 147-155.

Mind, 2013. [Online]
Available at: http://www.mind.org.uk/information-support/guides-to-support-and-services/advocacy-in-mental-health/

Missing Voices, 2012. *A review of independent professional advocacy services for looked after children and young people, care leavers and children in need in wales.* [Online]
Available at: www.childcomwales.org.uk/uploads/publications/283.pdf

Morris, J., 1999. Disabled children, Child protection systems and the Children Act 1989. *Child Abuse Review*, Volume 8, pp. 91-108.

Nadel, J. & Muir, D., 2005. *Emotional Development.* New York: Oxford University Press.

National Archives, 2010. [Online]
Available at: http://www.legislation.gov.uk/ukpga/1998/42/contents

Newell, P., 1991. *The UN Convention and Children's Rights in the UK.* London: National Children's Bureau.

Nice, 2014. [Online]
Available at: http://www.publications.nice.org.uk/quality-standard-for-the-health-and-wellbeing-of-looked-after-childre-and-young-people-gs31

NSPCC, n.d. *Speaking out 'A guide for advocates for children and young people with learning disabilities'.* [Online]
Available at: http://www.nspcc.org.uk/inform/publications/downloads/speakingout-wdf48015.pdf

Ofsted, 2014. [Online]
Available at: www.ofsted.gov.uk/schools

Parton, N., 2003. From Maria Colwell to Victoria Climbie: Reflections on a generation of public inquiries into child abuse. *Child Abuse Review.*

Parton, N. & Wattam, C., 1999. *Child Sexual Abuse (Responding to the Experiences of Children.* Chichester: John Wiley & Sons Ltd.

Save the Children, 2014. [Online]
Available at: http://www.savethechildren.org.uk/about-us/what-we-do/child-rights

Scope, 2014. [Online]
Available at: http://www.scope.org.uk/about-us/our-brand/social-model-of-disability

Scottish Government, 2009. *Child Protection Statistics.* [Online]
Available at:
http://www.scotland.gov.uk/Topics/Statistics/Browse/Children/TrendChildProtection

Stalker, K. & McArtgur, K., 2012. Child Abuse, Child Protection and Disabled Children: A review of recent research. *Child Abuse Review,* Volume 21, pp. 24-40.

Stein, M., 2009. *Quality Matters in Children's Services.* London: Jessica Kingsley Publishers.

The National Archives, 2010. [Online]
Available at: http://www.legislation.gov.uk/ukpga/1989/41/contents

Thomas, C., 2004. Developing the Social Relational in the Social Model of Disability: A theoretical agenda. *Implementing the Social Model of Disability: Theory and Research,* pp. 32-47.

UNICEF UK, 2012. [Online]
Available at: http://www.unicef.org.uk/Documents/Publications-pdfs/betterlifeleaflet2012_press.pdf

Utting, S. W., 1997. *People Like Us.* Norwich: Department Of Health.

www.ingramcontent.com/pod-product-compliance
Lightning Source LLC
Chambersburg PA
CBHW051422250726
48655CB00003B/1193